My First Chinese Picture Books for Short Sentences Book 4

我的第一套中文短句绘本 4

Xiaolin Huang

To Cooper and Danna for being the pilot readers

First Published in Australia in 2017
This edition published in 2017
by Xiaolin Huang
ABN 60 520 297 573

Copyright Xiaolin Huang 2017
127 Cambridge Cres
Wyndham Vale
VIC 3024, Australia

http://fb.me/mfcpb

National Library of Australia Cataloguing-in-Publication entry

Creator: Huang, Xiaolin, author.

Title: My first Chinese picture books for short sentences. Book 4 : 我的第一套中文短句绘本 第四册 / Xiaolin Huang.

ISBN: 9780648102540 (paperback)

Target Audience: For preschool age

Subjects: Chinese characters--Juvenile literature
Chinese language--Writing--Juvenile literature
Chinese language--Juvenile literature
Picture books for children

风车会转

救护车会救人

消防车会灭火

火车会在轨道上跑

直升机会在天上飞

小猫会抓老鼠

嘴巴会说话

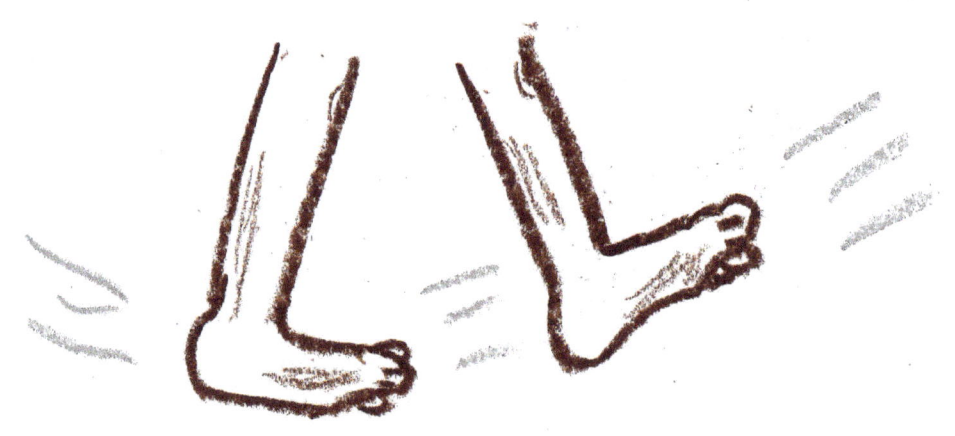

脚会走路

眼睛会看见东西

我会写中文字

我可以去游乐场吗？

我可以玩手机吗？

我可以看中文书吗?

小孩子可以开车吗？

大人可以开车吗?

小孩子可以坐飞机吗

大人可以坐飞机吗？

小孩子可以生火吗？

大人可以生火吗？

完

The End

本书常见字 你能认识几个

Frequently Used Characters
Try to recognise and read

火	生	走
风	见	刀
以	人	去
东	会	可
文	大	吗

www.ingramcontent.com/pod-product-compliance
Lightning Source LLC
Chambersburg PA
CBHW061822290426
44110CB00027B/2954